Ursula Andkjær Olsen
OUTGOING VESSEL

Translated by Katrine Øgaard Jensen

Photographic works by Sophia Kalkau

Action Books
Joyelle McSweeney and Johannes Göransson, Founding Editors
Katherine Hedeen and Paul Cunningham, Managing Editors
Austyn Wohlers, 2020-2021 Editorial Assistant
PJ Lombardo and Valerie Vargas, 2019-2020 Editorial Assistants
Jeffrey Angles, Daniel Borzutzky, Don Mee Choi, Advisory Board
Andrew Shuta, Book Design

Outgoing Vessel by Ursula Andkjær Olsen
Translated from the Danish by Katrine Øgaard Jensen

© 2021 Ursula Andkjær Olsen
Translation copyright © 2021 Katrine Øgaard Jensen

Originally published as *Udgående fartøj*
© 2015 Ursula Andkjær Olsen, Sophia Kalkau, and Gyldendal A/S

ISBN 978-0-900575-10-5
Library of Congress Control Number: 2020949108

Action Books, 233 Decio Hall, University of Notre Dame, IN, 46556 USA
actionbooks.org

Cover Design and Photographic Works: Sophia Kalkau

First Edition

With the generous support from:

Danish Arts
Foundation

OUTGOING VESSEL

I HAVE SPENT TIME

i have spent time interpreting/spreading dull perceptions
from my distant interior
deciphering them in their complexity
scattering them through time

that was a mistake
i should have worked to compress them further
until they became stone

the hermetically sealed
the unreachable
the lost

it's time to launch it all

The processing of - grief
                  - existence
                  - the world

no one except me can hate feelings
anyone else who claims to hate feelings:
let it be known how they still succumb to them
anyone else who claims to hate feelings:
let it be known how they, in weak moments
open up to them and

and become soft with longing

among all time's winners
i am the hardest

just-meet-some-people-lovers
authenticity-lovers
spontaneity-lovers
symbiosis-lovers
heart-lovers
body-lovers

cry your tears
cry your snot
cry your blood
cry your piss

out with it

like when i
AT night
in moonshine
enter a garden of marble
between ornamented walls
walk to a basin in the floor
and it turns out
there is no space in the basin
for what i need to unload
there is no FUCKING space

i can't get the knot to disappear, but i can strip it of its
distinction by molding it into the hard, smooth material
that i have molded everything else into

it will be like so:
an interior
mine
filled with wholly smooth, wholly identical
orbs

is hate smooth and does it encircle disjointed love
is love smooth and does it encircle disjointed hate

i don't think disjointed is the word i'm looking for

i no longer want to
search for words

i sneer at all of you intimacy-lovers
i sneer at all of you love-lovers
i sneer at all of you nurture-lovers

i don't want your authenticity
i don't want your tastefulness
i don't want your true emotions
i don't want your indignation and engagement

i want to BATHE in pure sentimentality
to CLEANSE MYSELF in pure sentimentality

MY body SCREAMS for sentimentality
a hard, smooth material
i can be molded into

ASIDE FROM THAT THERE IS NOTHING TO GET
AND NOTHING WILL COME

I laugh at all lovers
I laugh at all love-lovers
I laugh at all of you ignorant-lovers

I detest your authenticity
I detest your taste for life
I detest your genuine emotions
I detest your concern and engagement

I want to be rid of all sentiments
to cleanse myself in stoicism

the disjointed hate-love
the disjointed system of hate-love
open/closed
WIDE OPEN
what should i cover it with?
the disjointed assigns the body an impossible task:
to hold it together

the tough and necessary upbringing toward hardness
the tough and necessary upbringing toward hardness
the tough and necessary upbringing toward hardness

your additive worldview
is math without the infinite
without a zero point

i have to spell it out in stone
metal
work with what i've got

i cut too hard, they can't have me work with flesh and blood
they just can't, it would be a bloodbath, not with these soft things
all things, i can't with the lives and feelings of others, only my
own feelings are hard enough, i'll have to spell it out in stone
metal

cut it out

they can't have me speak with the undisciplined, i would
cut too hard, i can only talk to myself, only my own feelings are
hard enough

i will worship discipline
as a divine method
i will whip myself
not for pleasure, not at all, but for greatness
i will achieve it
and then i will hate all things weak, soft, anything
breakable

two dogs are tangled up in each other's leashes in front of me
at the park, which leads to my point: not the disjointed, but the
discordant, consisting of different agents pulling in different
directions and STILL not coming apart: a knot of dogs

that knot is what i'm talking about
that knot should probably be molded into a hard, smooth
material

it always becomes a pattern
so let it become a hard pattern

among all winners

the blind winner
the happy winner
the pretty winner
the stupid winner
the evil winner
the babbling winner
the batshit winner
the sore winner

out of all time's winners
i am the hard one

predator and fortress in one

the faculty of hardness
feeling joy in the faculty itself and
feeling joy in its many applications

in a community
in my treatment of myself and others

no one should forgive me
nor those who sin against me
i am unforgivable

AS ARE THOSE WHO SIN AGAINST ME

the lie glows on a background of suppression
the truth glows on a background of suppression
anything that glows
anything that used to glow
anything that will ever glow
will do so on a background of suppression

the demand for hardness glows on a background of
suppression, of all that is breakable

the demand for hardness is irreconcilable

the loser is an animal
the winner is an animal
the one who watches the loser from above is a winner
the one who watches the winner from above is

is a

knot
in a sarcophagus
in a pyramid
in a desert of uselessness

to my victims i say:

it is your job to hate me
do your job and hate me
and do what must be FUCKING done
you are not capable of doing what must be FUCKING done
I'LL DO IT MYSELF

LOSERS

i've said it before
i'll say it again:

come here and peek into my power apparatus

LOSERS

i refuse to admit that i want people's forgiveness
i refuse to admit that i want people's
i refuse to admit that i want people
i will deny it

i will fake my way to pity, recognition, attention

love
also love

and
forgiveness

appreciation AS a virus that my immune system will attack
without mercy

my arrogance AS a sphere of light that surrounds me
when i dance

to know that hardness creates the best results
the most absolute results

to inherently know that hardness isn't an option
only partially an option

to know that being economical with love isn't an option

unable to blame myself
when being economical with love isn't an option

deploy everyone

stick the breast in the mouth and breathe

deploy everyone: mom, dad, little sister, loved one, child

the luxury of indecision
the anxiety of indecision

i stick my breast in my mouth and breathe
there's the solution
the soul as THE hollow suction in the stomach
it hollows
in the stomach

LOSS AND THE CLOAKING OF LOSS
LOSS AND THE CLOAKING OF LOSS

with a hard, smooth material
with a blue silk robe

i am not in touch with my existence on a daily basis
i am not present in my body
not a single fucking thing happens when i dream

it's time to launch it all

identification with one's own emotionalism
identification with one's own dissociation from the emotional

not total and yet
not possible to escape

let it be written:
hate yourself
as you hate your neighbor

to honor and protect hardness
to beat it into something harder until it is pulverized
to mix the powder with crystal-clear water
and drink it
and mold a new human out of the clay
from the inside

there are no pictures here
nothing looks like anything else, everything is enclosed

this is a shape i cannot remain in

technoscientific1

revenge is upon us
just below the skin, she's ready
hairs stand up, chopped, vertical
full fear-regalia

yes, says yes-doll to no-doll: take your
silk and come here and
lower your body into relaxing water

i'm in total dread-regalia
i play dice in my silk on a shimmering lake

he, revenge
single-celled under the skin
like a cave that SITS ready
below the heart.

After ward we fall into a swamp of changes.

yes, says the doll, no: Keyword
Nourishment-Noise.
Silk Lower Your body Into the Flaccid water.

I'm in maximum horror-regalia.
A Remix dresses ME in my silk and plays chuck-a-luck
on the lake.

Yes-doll says to no-doll:
Lower your body.

It SITS ready, The Distant.
Single-Celled, under the skin.

It SITS ready, The Distant.

Single-Celled, under the skin.

Yes-Doll Says to No-Doll:
Silk of the day.

Yes-doll says to no-doll: just put on your
Silk and come down here and
Lower your flabby body

in all its terror-regalia.
I put on my silk and roll the dice

after ward we fell

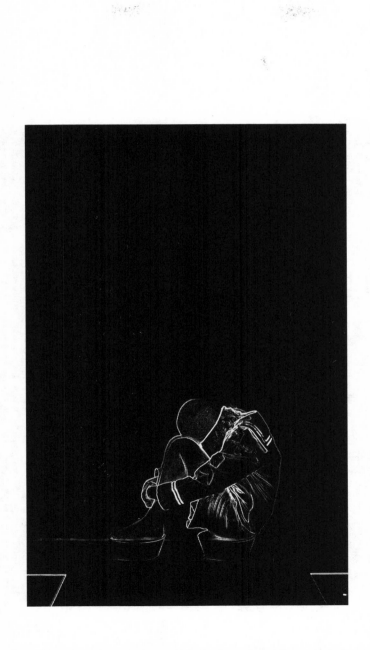

I PERCEIVE SELF-HATE AS A NECESSARY SKILL

self-hate is not a psychological state
self-hate is an attitude i deem necessary

destructive is my normal state

the sand is soft with longing
the sea is soft with longing
humankind is soft with longing

the sand has hardened with longing
the sea has hardened with longing
humankind has hardened with longing

to regard safety as a positive trait
to regard wealth as a positive trait
to regard luck as a positive trait
coziness as a personal quality
in line with safety and wealth

and luck

to flaunt the above

to have a good and rich *face*
to have a *feel-good* personality

your staggering lack of self-hate
your intolerable lack of self-hate
your unacceptable lack of self-hate

your unacceptable, additive worldview

my path to destruction is via self-destruction
my path to the destruction of everything that MUST
be destroyed is via self-destruction
my path to the necessary destruction of all that MUST
be destroyed is via exercises in self-destruction

self-destructions are but études (military exercises)

REMEMBER

the actual annihilation will also destroy those
who must be destroyed

i enter my own spring, and in there i do it
i do all that is necessary
all the killings that must be committed
i commit in there

i enter my own terrible spring, and in there i do it
i do all that is necessary
all the births that must be committed
i commit in there

it is me i kill
it is NOT me i give birth to

in there i do it:

that movement wherein loser becomes winner
becomes

that movement wherein the winner again becomes
loser becomes avenger
becomes

the new human

i use ALL PARTS OF the feeling
AS i would use ALL PARTS OF my prey

i have become more calculating

by slipping this
into the body
screwing it into the socket
letting it grow and hate
whatever must be hated
letting it lash out from inside
bringing it into the world

to want experience
is to want the destruction of yourself from inside/outside
get with it

i have no respect for people who don't hate themselves, people who don't hate themselves disgust me, people who don't hate themselves are not people

autonomy but NOT as NOT thinking of others
autonomy as ruthlessness toward power
insofar as possible
autonomy as ruthlessness toward one's own lack of power
insofar as possible

the necessary suicide:
to board the orb
buckle in
to send off the hating i

first AS escape, then AS
resurrection

dear ones: without self-hate, no autonomy, no dark
only those who hate themselves truly
are capable of hating others, are capable of
darkness and autonomy
now you know

you have mistaken blindness for darkness
you have mistaken blindness for darkness
you have mistaken blindness for darkness

the rich dark
the lone light

the goal is to have a personality type that feels fortified
and justified, perhaps even revived and delivered
when met with resistance, reluctance, scorn and derision

is the goal to have a personality type that feels fortified
and justified, perhaps even revived and delivered
when met with resistance, reluctance, scorn and derision?

the hope to

always feel fortified and justified

to not have a personality

what big eyes i have
the better to hate me with
what big ears i have
the better to hate me with
what a terrible big mouth i have
the better to eat me with

it is no one else's doing
i am eating myself up from within
restlessly

as mentioned
i have closed myself around itself
in a closed circuit
/orb
which i will send off as the outgoing
vessel that it is
after which the new human can arrive in its

incoming

the precision of a prayer is crucial

the ant will be my totem animal
i hate ants
they must be me
and i must be them
i pray that:

i can carry my own weight 100 times
i can survive under water for several hours
my exoskeleton renders me practically immortal
beneath my exoskeleton a whole world exists, the whole world
my exterior is the celestial concave that my interior needs

everything sings

i give zero fucks about death
i will think of nothing but growth

re: pathos
that's what i will do

i will do it
and then i will beat it
drag it through the dirt
sully it
taunt it
and then do it all again

emotions
not as confession
not as experiment but

as discipline

ALL PARTS OF the feeling

all gifts must be avenged
each and every one

i have become more calculating

this is mathematically necessary
and also how it should feel:

a destruction of the human
that came before this experience
that's also how i feel
all experience is destruction
a necessary destruction of what came before
that's also how i feel

IT IS NECESSARY TO HATE YOURSELF

HOW ELSE WOULD I BE ABLE TO HATE EVERYONE
WHO NEEDS TO BE HATED?

how else would the new human emerge?

the hand
you hate yourself with

how else would the new human emerge?

(the hand
you love yourself with)

every statement is a postulate about universality

every statement
like the very idea of reaching beyond yourself
across the marketplace
is a postulate

people who aren't willing to withdraw their statements

people who don't hate themselves have no right
people who aren't willing to kill themselves to become new
humans
have no right

I WILL LIFT UP MY COUNTENANCE UPON YOU
AND GIVE YOU SHIT

it's time

i must withdraw this statement
i must withdraw this statement
i must withdraw this statement
i must withdraw this statement

*technoscientific***2**

do not think i will fragilize myself for you
do not think i am interested in your fragilization of yourself
know that i am in command of almost 100 percent of myself
know that i have stowed away my last uncontrollables

in my bones
in my limbs
in my bullet- and waterproof armor
it cannot escape

so that when evening slaughters me and eats me and
finds the orb, it will never find it

fear not

know that i am not interested in curbing you

that i voluntarily and independently
have planted it in my interior
that it is growing
that one day it will fill my entire interior
that one day it will have taken over and i will
be someone else

in in the cyst's
birth of something else
i-dust
i

to
to dust
in the bones, so that when you slaughter me every evening
you will never notice

the mother's bones
the I-DISTURBANCE
the i's breast/dream

i-dust
to
to
must i

know that i have stowed away my uncontrollables
in my, iiin life's bones
in a coffin
in the dust
in

so that when i slaughter myself every evening and eat
the meat and find the orb, I will never find it
it is crucial that i never find it

MY VACUUM IS HIDDEN
WHERE NO ONE CAN EVER FIND IT
LIKE A PLANET WITHIN

evening slaughters me and eats me
and leaves the orb in the dark
it will never find anything
in the bones of my beloveds
in the cysts

in the dust

in
in

THE PRECISION OF A PRAYER

prayer as talking sense to yourself
as starting in one place and ending in another

a useful way to
exchange the abyss in yourself for shame
exchange life's emptiness for scarcity
exchange

change abyss to surface
change the void to anger
it always becomes a pattern, so let it be a hard one
and change anger to revenge

prayer as talking sense to yourself
prayer as talking sense to yourself
change abyss to revenge to a hard pattern
to start in one place and end in another
no
to start in one place and end in the same place
change
start in one place and end in the same place
void to void
revenge to revenge
no
to
no

i don't know WHAT this is
i cry all the time
it is NOT normal
what even is the point
i've taken asthma medication to see if it helps
water in the lungs
dust in the lungs
hate in the lungs

SOMETHING in my lungs THAT SHOULD NOT BE THERE

the wound itself is NOTHING
it's NOT about the wound that was inflicted on me
it's NOT about the wound that i will probably inflict
on the wounders/humiliators
PAIN as such, FUCK IT
revenge is about total humiliation of those who humiliate me
who have humiliated me

BECAUSE i let myself be humiliated
let myself be wounded

humiliation does not need bloodshed
humiliation will work differently
humiliation will color the blood piss-yellow, color the wounds
piss-yellow

everywhere from inside

they will walk around in the world
brightly piss-yellow inwardly/outwardly
a color that will ring like plaguebells
walk around bright with stench, bright with humiliation
ALWAYS visible

NEVER SHIELDED

i am an adult human being
by my own wish

i am an adult human being
do not call me uncompromising
do not call me free

there is something wrong with my skin
it has not lived up to my expectations
i refuse to take my skin seriously

what i expected: for the skin to shield, encircle everything
like a protective layer, ensure that i felt waterproof, it should
be waterproof, proof in every way

it has not done its job
who can take skin like that seriously
it is a laughable organ that should be replaced with
something else, gold for instance

prayer as talking sense to yourself

is there anyone who would like me to talk sense to them?
is there anyone else who would like me to talk sense to them?

THERE IS SOMETHING WRONG WITH MY EMOTIONS

i am an adult adult adult adult adult adult adult adult adult adult human being do not shit on my loss with your young shit

that it's a sign of health to always see yourself
from the outside

that it's a sign of health to have the ability
to always see yourself from the outside

that it's a sign of health to have the ability
to always see yourself from the outside, even though
it feels like a loss, because the absence of
this ability is an even greater loss

a loss of the hand
that you hold yourself with

a loss of the arm with the hand
that you hold yourself with

a loss of the body with the arm with the hand
that you hold yourself with

a loss of the other
that you hold yourself with

a loss of the other
that you hold yourself with

it is a far-out ability
people's ability to take themselves seriously

it is a terrible ability
people's ability to take themselves seriously

(atonement-fear)
(atonement-flight)

the self not AS monolith
the self AS relation

prayer AS
prayer AS

i'll wait by the elevator

hate is natural, lawful and necessary
or
hate is an expression of the highest freedom

self-hate is
self-hate is

the true value of hate lies in the guilt it's connected to

to control this guilt is to control EVERYTHING

the precision of a prayer

to hate yourself AND let yourself live
to hate AND let live

that is the goal

i am completely without empathy
i cannot feel anything/anyone

from this zero point
what emerges is ANGER
the first thing that emerges every fucking time
is ANGER
it rips loose
AS THE FIRST THING

from this zero point
i imagine the other feelings
grow out
rip loose

that's what i hope

i am sick because everything is sick
i have to come up with something
because i am sick
inwardly/outwardly
what do i envision
my approach is not that easy
fuck
i don't see any images in my day to day
where is my easy approach
how am i supposed to arrive

my approach is

I HAVE TO COME UP WITH EVERYTHING MYSELF
NOTHING I'VE SEEN CAN SAVE ME

prayer is talking sense to yourself
never pray for the impossible
never pray for the impossible
never pray for the impossible
pray for the impossible

i must be forced into love

i will piss on my loss

like the elderly asshole that i am
like the elderly person that i am
on a big, smooth floor, covered in sleek
orbs

here i will roll around
here my elderly ass will tumble
here I will piss on MY loss with my OWN old piss

everyone must love me

the precision of a prayer is crucial

to walk into the alienated space
and sit in the center of the covered market
to sit in the center of the alienated space
under a roof of glass
and feel as close to the authentic as
those close to suffering
are

the authentic space doesn't reveal itself
due to the concealment of something else
suffering
alienation

the authentic space is suffering and alienation in one image

not just the suffering
not just the alienated

these thoughts ran past me
in front of me, into another space
with other two-faced walls

suffering is the source
alienation is the mouth
suffering is the source
alienation is the mouth

this is the prayer behind clinical language:
remove every feeling

this IS a prayer
this IS NOT a neutral wish

i will do it as quietly as i can
i will be an effective angel

(this cannot be erased
all wounds will be erased)

you must all become friends with MY shame
it turns everyone into siblings

i must become friends with YOURS

that is the goal

this is my task
no one else will take it
i say:
the path of corruption, compromise
is also the path of self-denial
the path of mystery
get with it

i am a donkey that must be shameridden
i am an animal that must be loved shamelessly
by the shameless

the soft part will become scheming
the hard part will be beside itself
my openness will grow
where the walls were
there will be nothing
but locked doors left
my mental architecture AS total chaos

deploy everyone

no one will find the path
all ARE out and in
all ARE cut out and cut in
all ARE silkrobed in blue

everyone needs love

technoscientific3

life in the coffin
refuge for the human
the human in the empty space

The Thing.
Life.

the things in the breast
refuge in the empty space inside the human

rights in the breast
a refuge
a coffin
with in humans

human nature
in the coffin, a
relic, collection of Bones and Hair
encapsulated and stored in
a humane vacuum..

this is
the refuge

the human refusing to let go

something to shout into the void
with in

Life / *death*
humans

humans in the empty space

life

In the coffin a
holiness in the empty space
inside the humane.

A Door.
Life.

a life in the jewel box
the jewel box in the human
the human In the empty space.

The Thing ..
Life.

The Thing in the jewel box
the jewel box in the empty space in the human-
human.

The Thing in the jewel box
the jewel box in the human
encapsulated and stored.

With bones and hair

This is About a
holiness in
inside the human.

Something to shout into the void..
What the human Refuses to let go of.

The Scream in
inside the human-
humans.

The Thing in this scream

Lifedeath in
in the humans.

The Scream iin
The Human in the open DOORWAY.

THE THING.
Liife.

iiin

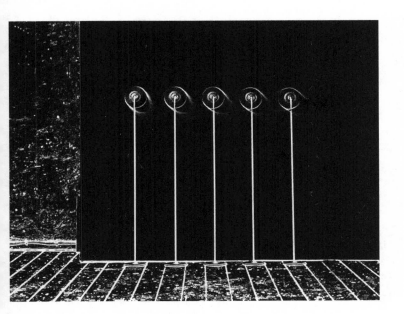

I PERFORM ENCAPSULATIONS

the human
the wish to be virgin once again
the wish to have never said a word
to be stingy with one's openings
to tie oneself in a knot

i tied myself in a knot
and there stands the human

/the orb

i send you this
a mobile statue/sarcophagus

an outgoing vessel

the emotional state is key to the overall
painexperience

I DO NOTHING

the coagulated human
lovely at last
in its outgoing vessel

what if i invited the body to act differently
what if it didn't tense up

whenever it
whenever i see something beautiful
it feels like giving in

what if i didn't tense up

that is NOT an option

what is left when i set my feelings aside:
a negative imprint of them
just as obvious as before

a coffin that grows inside me

we must assume there is an original alienation:
first the estrangement, a person, a stranger to themselves
stranger to others, the person exists deep inside their
distant interior, without knowing, they must escape to the
surface, from inside, to become human

the agony that is created
not when they sound the human/body
but when they lift their hand/relieve the pressure
that had just been placed on a particular
organ, such as the appendix

and the pain pours out
from all its ducts

painducts

what if the moon is facing away from earth
and has given us its back all along
the agony of it

i'm seeing white

the mother who birthed nothing
and cut it off from everything
who carried it under her heart
where it sits now
where it grows again
that mother
will continue birthing
nothing, will always cut
the cord, every month
the mother will cut the cord
and trigger the delicate circulation of nothing
again
every month she will
overcome the fear of separation
and, against her wishes
set nothing free

LET IT BE KNOWN THAT EVERYTHING AND NOTHING
CAN NEVER BE SEPERATED
WILL ALWAYS MEET AGAIN

a mentalhygienic relationship that results in the body being
cleansed away
the body is dirt that must be washed off the spirit

a bodyhygienic relationship that results in the spirit being
cleansed away
the spirit is dirt that must be washed off the body

the generality of both options
the generality of the losses that both options present

the individual aspect of the chosen option

the fact that it CAN be thrown out
means that it is of paramount importance
to have it thrown out

vulnerable like a
crummy prosthetic leg with the skin flaking off

human like a
crummy prosthetic leg with the skin flaking off

i have decided to gather all vulnerability in my body
it will make my spirit invulnerable

there is something about my body
what is it
it cannot hang around there, in the back
the most vulnerable of vulnerable bodies
cannot sit in there
it could mean salvation
if there IS NOT a body BACK THERE
it's interesting, i am working on the assumption
that there is a moat all around
could it be?
it is me
and behind it
i am there again like an infinite row of open doors
you can tumble right through
EVERYONE can, i've said it before
the vulnerable is an incredibly narrow area
like an onion layer, no matter which one
you can keep going in and in
to find me
as unplaceable as power
in the third-millennium heart
just as unplaceable
is what i will be

BUT WE CAN WEAVE TOGETHER OUR MOATS
AND EVERYONE CAN SAIL AMONG EACH OTHER
IN THE CANAL SYSTEM THAT IS CREATED
THAT IS ALREADY HERE
THE NEW ONTOLOGY

you must open your moats to mine
stretch your canals into my abyss

what's inside the doll when you peel off the outer layer, when
its surface cracks and you think to yourself: there will be
nothing left once the skin has crumbled; that nothing is what
you will have to find

touch

something bursts
and something else gets out

i am crushed under the rubble

i perform the necessary encapsulations of
what is lost
what was not there
what SHOULD HAVE BEEN
i take immediate action

first i consume what is lost
read: the dead
it is an indigestible meal
it is a nondegradable meal
then i'll have a foundation

inwardly

on which i can build myself

INSIDE ME THERE IS A NONDEGRADABLE ORB
MY OWN PLANET

desert of nondegradability

i can learn to smile hard
look people in the eye without smiling at them
i will be rewarded for it
i must not make for myself any carved images
i must not smile at people
i will utilize other ornaments

my concealing wall will be full of images
my concealing wall will be made of gold
behind this image-bearing AND concealing wall of gold is
all that must be kept out of view
there lies the orb
i am occupied with everything material
the material as in unreachable

devour all meat and expose the bones

/the orb

that smile in my body like a knot

i prefer to dress my own wounds, it's the safest
way to know it's been done properly

i prefer to perform my own encapsulations, it's the safest
way to know it's been done properly

i am completely without empathy
it happens to me frequently
i am not evil
i just can't feel anything/anyone

(in my body like a knot)

those who say that water
is doing grief's work

back and forth:

grief-enhancing
grief-inhibiting
suppression-enhancing
suppression-inhibiting

washing
massaging
touching
cradling
letting it stream through

THEY'RE LYING

those who say:

a life ends
like grass tread flat
a scent at the border of consciousness

THEY'RE LYING

a desert of nondegradability
a desert of uselessness

in that i trust

in the desert lies a pyramid
in the pyramid lies a sarcophagus
in the sarcophagus lies an orb
WHICH is the foundation of all future life
WHICH is the new path to the necessary virginity

a shaft
my own shaft of longing
with my own shaft of loss

i'll wait for you by the elevator

i wish i were born still
in still water

LIKE the human/orb

LIKE seconds
that just stay inside me
the way i stay inside me

is defiance of death a feeling close to life
at the source of life
is defiance of death a feeling far from life
at the border of life

is the source or the mouth closest to life
the river

death-angst
death-hate
death-resistance

those with orb-shaped eggs
are my family

the streaming in your mom
the streaming in your dad
the streaming in your little sister
the streaming in your loved one
the streaming in your child

to talk yourself into seeing the streaming
to look into your own eyes and see the streaming

to look into your mom's eyes and see the streaming
to look into your dad's eyes and see the streaming
to look into your little sister's eyes and see the streaming
to look into your loved one's eyes and see the streaming
to look into your child's eyes and see the streaming

look at them stream away

YOU must look into YOUR children's eyes and see it

look your children in the eyes and get with it
must i look my child in the eyes and get it
the already=not=my=child
in the eyes of MY child

MUST I

DEPLOY EVERYONE

those with orb-shaped eggs
who are swaddled in delicate
silk crepe woven souls

those with orb-shaped eggs
are my family

my loss is in the right place

the beloved object
IN a cocoon somewhere inside
refusing to let go of the beloved object and placing it
IN a cocoon somewhere inside
refusing to let go of the beloved object, which has already
been lost WHO KNOWS WHERE, and placing it
IN a cocoon somewhere inside

IT'S THE BUTTERFLY WHOSE COCOON IS ROUND
LIKE AN ORB
THE LOSS IS THAT DUMBASS BUTTERFLY WHOSE
COCOON IS ROUND AND HARD LIKE AN ORB

i am a stonehard orb-bearer
i am a stonehard orb-bearer
i am a stonehard orb-bearer

do not come to me with your soft shit

my hand is incapable of shaking
i want my hand to shake

inside the orb there is NOTHING
just letting you know
rocks all the way, marble, granite, basalt
ALL THE WAY

that's how virginity is, not empty, not anything
a non-complex lifeform
solid all the way
nothing to see here

you can let it lie, stand
let it overgrow with moss
whatever it is
that grows

IN THAT LANDSCAPE
virginity lies in the sand like a pyramid
in its depths lies the orb
in its FUCKING sarcophagus

THERE IS NOTHING FOR YOU TO FIND

no one can ever
discover who i am

does this mean:

no one can ever discover
the streaming

or

no one can ever discover
what lies behind the stream

like a stonehard orb

someone i know has lost
some loser i know

to lose all you have
to lose all you have had
to be the loser of all you had

to lose
to have lost
to be a loser

to lose AND HAVE TO BEAR YOUR LOSS
to lose AND HAVE TO BEAR THAT YOU HAVE
FUCKING LOST
to lose AND HAVE TO BEAR WHAT YOU HAVE
FUCKING LOST

like a hard orb
hard orb

sitting in its hole under the heart

pangeaic in its might
IN ALL ITS PANGEAIC MIGHT
LIKE A GLOBAL DESERT
AN ABSOLUTE HALLELUJAH

to have a memory
to have natural access to your memory
to have unnatural access to your memory

to have no access to your memory

to have the entrance to your memory sealed

forever

i am a

all-is-hermetically-sealed-lover
all-is-inaccessible-lover
all-is-lost-lover

my untouchability is my core
my distant interior is my core
my lack of closeness is my core

so many dead
their eyeballs are filling this vessel

grave
vessel
grave
vessel

the earth is a slow fire

re: counting the dead:

i have a strategy in place
I HAVE A STRATEGY IN PLACE

to roll a burning wheel down a hill like a solar symbol
to roll a tenacious orb down a hill like a
like a
like a

longing moves in all directions
like a sphere of light that scatters around me
i brush my hair in its circle

to be more concise:
human longing scatters like a
BIG BANG around it

around the human
in the wet grass
hair

it's this BIG BANG that must be reversed
to its original condition, an infinitely heavy orb;
must be molded into a hard, smooth material
and placed in the hole below the heart

where it must remain

i have bound my ties in a
STONEHARD MATERIAL
it's taken 1,000 years inside
i have wrung myself to create
the necessary loop

wrungness caused by external violence
wrungness caused by the exercise of violence
wrungness caused by flight
wrungness caused by care

it's all there, in the loop created
when i lay my head in my lap

and close the gate

these are my bonehard illusions
i want to break their necks
i want a clean death

a conscious movement AWAY from the flesh
fucking away from it
fucking flesh
get with it

ANYTHING BUT this natural dissipation

i think of the automat as monolith: the transforming principle
as something WHOLLY pure, WHOLLY inaccessible
NOT a machine that lets the material go through a
transformation process of which you can follow every part
but a transformation in ONE blow

that's what i want

ALL must be put through that automat
ALL must be transformed
ALL must be smooth as – WHAT IS
SUFFICIENTLY SMOOTH?

I must become as smooth as the smoothest in the world
I must become as smooth as the smoothest in the world

to have marble skin
not as an invitation
but as a bulwark
the strongest there is
the most comfortable
the sacrosanctest

untouchablest

i'm thinking of training my body
until it becomes a rock
that is my objective
the most precise expression of it

it's better to cut a new one,
to cut anew, and hew from it
a perfect orb
any shape i want
hew from it a
rectangle, cube, almond, moon
AND THEN move in
once it's done

to cut it out
to bring forward its complexity of interior and exterior

and then perform a ritual that brings resistance to suffering
where you can view
the suffering/human in a scale of 1:1
and the shape that the human must resist with
which is
the suffering/human in a scale of infinite:infinite

to dress it in a blue silk robe
of hard, smooth material

the loss is absolutely real and absolutely unreal
all that must be experienced is unreal
until it has been experienced
if it can be experienced
not everything can be

that is why: you can come home
every day

MANY EXPERIENCES POORER

i am sorry for my loss
i am sorry for my loss
i am sorry for my loss
i am sorry for my loss

all experience is pathetic
all use of language is in itself a prayer

NO MATTER WHAT YOU SAY

the immortal I
the heart hidden in a drop-shaped jewel box
hidden in the blood it pumps around itself

the immortal II
the loss hidden in the egg
hidden in the fish
hidden in the whale
hidden in the sea
hidden in its own abyss

immanence is not a monolith
transcendence IS an abyss

loss IS a monolith
loss IS an abyss
loss IS a monolith in its own abyss

i am against death
i am against death
i am against death

first it is necessary to have hidden something
then it can be acknowledged that something
has been hidden
then it can be acknowledged that it must have significance
since it was hidden
finally, it can be acknowledged that everything depends
on this very something being
hidden

first it is necessary to have remembered something
then it can be acknowledged that something
has been remembered
then it can be acknowledged that it must have significance
since it was remembered
finally, it can be acknowledged that everything depends
on this very something being
remembered

there is a period, between the moment when the something
was first hidden/remembered
and the moment when its importance was acknowledged
in which time moves in all directions

I am the great remoteness-ideologist

humans are something exterior to me
i am something exterior to me, can i
use that?

that must be good for something or

i exit into the unreal

let the complex and non-complex lifeforms
come to me

there is a being
hidden in every stone

there is a stone
hidden in every being

*technoscientific***4**

i am NOT inviting the body to act differently
the coagulated human
in its outgoing vessel

confined at last
closed at last
(strategically dammed)

the coagulated human
NOT as NOT thinking of others
INsofar as possible
exercising ruthlessness toward power
INsofar as possible
exercising ruthlessness toward one's own lack of power
my self as an outgoing vessel as
sleeping in an outgoing vessel
SO alien
SO lonely
SO frozen

SO dreamy

NEVER BEFORE SO CALM

that is MY hyperdream
do not disturb me in MY hyperdream

c'est mon rêve trop
calme
j'ai interrompu
mon rêve n'est pas terminée
je suppose que mon rêve très
calme est trop
calme

je mérite de ressentir ce que vous ressentez
l'amour
vous m'avez envoyé un visage de
calme

I sat in nostalgia
And said: my heart is sitting there, there, there, there, there

triste, nostalgique
je dis: vous, le plus rouge-rouge
changements de personnalité, là, là, là, là et là.

changes in the nature of the face

so steady
so hypothetical
never before so quiet

I say: it is beautiful, and it will be Red

Mother's Kind..

this is my TOO calm dream
i was interrupted
i am cross cruel
there, there, there, there
there

my dream IS not finished
i was Interrupted
i assume that my calm dream is TOO calm
i deserve to feel what you feel
LOVE

the mother sent me a Calm Face..

space, which is black, blackblue
and the numb gliding
still lovely
the coagulated human
in its outgoing
lovely at last

like when something bursts and..
the dome, breath's temple collapses and
something else is crushed under the rubble

like when something bursts and
something else escapes the dome, gets out of that
temple, out

what, who,

the feeling is crushed Under the rubble
the feeling escapes and becomes itself out in the air

like an Outgoing vessel

and i become myself out in the air

do i know anything worth knowing
do i feel anything worth feeling

(love)

you were sent as a friendly face
under the moon,

i will sleep IN outer space
i was made FOR low pressure

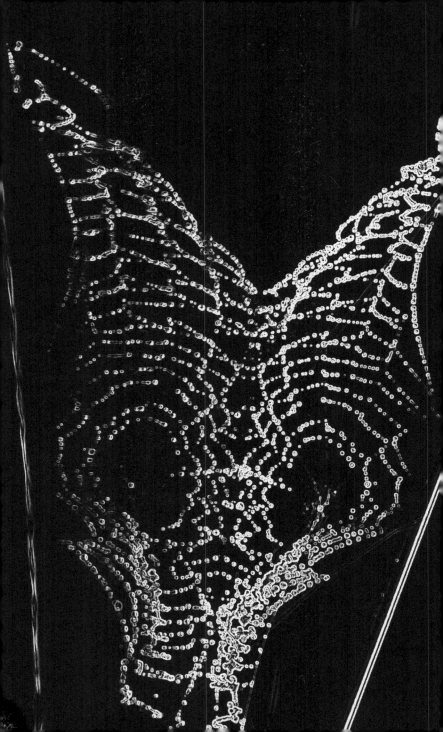

TECHOSCIENTIFICSALVATION

utopia as an exit/entrance
as the very concept of getting out/in

paradise as a vessel IN the world with an exit/entrance
as the very concept of being able to get out/in
as the very concept of having a vessel
with ornamented walls
with a basin in the floor

strong BUT smooth
light BUT cold

loss has an inside
loss should have an inside

i do the necessary work on the walls
i do the necessary work on the floor

i get in

deploy with everyone

my goal is to invalidate ALL loneliness
my goal is to communicate WITH EVERYTHING

i launch the orb as an outgoing/incoming vessel
i have slowly begun to break out of my isolation
the inhuman is not unfriendly

i have started working on my softer parts
i have started communicating through body expansions

touch screen
looking glass
touch screen
looking glass

/orb

i will erect the new paradise
i will build and decorate it
LIKE a garden in an outgoing/incoming vessel
with ornamented walls
with a basin in the floor

it is made from light and pleasant materials
on the walls, lifeforms stand out in relief
i can feel them ALL when i stroke the wall with my hands
on the basin floor, lifeforms stand out in relief
the lifeforms of water
i can feel them ALL when i cross the bottom with my bare
feet

i can feel EVERYTHING

lifeforms
AND
deathforms

i want to create it
like an orb with touch screen/looking glass
all is inside that orb, the whole world
i want to build it out of light and pleasant materials
inside it are also the dead
they emerge as images on its smooth surface
which can be covered in grass
in one motion the orb can be covered in grass
and whatever you want
the dead
EVERYTHING, EVERYONE will grow out from its surface

i am growing on you
you are growing on me
everyone is growing on everyone

to cut it out
to bring forward its complexity of interior and exterior

to insert the hearts

to spend time inside it
to see that it is incomplete
because it must be a home for humans once it's done
to see that it is good

the sum of all hearts is in itself a heart
IT BEATS

the sum of all realities is in itself
REAL

IT BEATS

to some
to name and to love is the same
to name and to love

that is why i will leave
this earth

DEPLOY EVERYONE

i don't know much about this landscape
the light is filled with dust
there's a staircase in the middle

the land is obscured in the searing light
i walk up the stairs, upward, to the light
at the top

i see:
the desert
the pyramid
the sarcophagus
the orb

i see it all

to remember is to love
to

bathe
anoint
swaddle

the heart/brain so it becomes an
outgoing/incoming

with ornamented
with a basin

i send it to you

with ornamented walls
AS love-surfaces
AS exo-organ

allowing all users access to several
separate parts of each other – at the same time
allowing all users to engage with each other's
surfaces – at the same time
omens and wonders will bring us to the next world

LIKE pain-surfaces

humans MUST have been meant to be
more conscious of pain
humans MUST have been meant to be
more conscious of – their own and others' – pain

and then alleviate it

the radicality of experience
the radicality of empathy
the radicality of experience
the radicality of empathy
the radicality of experience
the radicality of empathy

i want to journey out/into it all

meet me there

*technoscientific***5**

the garden AS a power symbol conveying control over earth
where elegant structures mirror nature's riches
A Carved stone garden in the inner walls of the temple
Is there a swimming pool, rather than the floor?
I think there is a pool instead of the floor.

the garden is heaven iitself!
the earth raised . out. of time

god built a garden
and put humans in it
and threw them out again, nono

the Garden of eden . was. made by human hands
ONE carved stone .-
garden in the inner walls. Of . the temple
Is there a swimmingpool, *rather than the floor?*
I think there is!

the human built a garden
to meet god
who came to that garden
who liked to take a stroll in there
and feel the evening air against their cheeks

the human built a garden FOR god
AS an intimate portrait of god,
where he/she/they get to enjoy the cool evening air
against their cheek, in their garden
and then give the human permission
to look after and care for it
(bathe anoint swaddle)

the garden's true resident
god / queen / king / gardener / yesyesyes

helps us find the actual garden
a rising number of specific sources

that supply the garden
with current

The Earth himself
AS refuge
To take a stroll in Heaven YOURSELF a STROLL
LIKE children in the evening air
LIKE two times god That was my role in the garden

the garden of the self is the sky!
, Gott zu begegnen
, Die in den Garten kam

the entrance is guarded by terrible, mystic beings,
CHERUB/sphinx
we do not talk about the fact
that beasts are guarding the garden

eden IS not at the creation of the world
it is a queen / king /loser in their temple
atTRacting Loss with their KIND
how can a temple, be , a garden?
a Temple can easily be a garden!

beängstigend, geheimnisvolle Wesen
einsame Mensch im Turm der krig

Verbunden sind all Schiffe

ALS Kosmos
zu seinen Göttern

status-quo-god

A garden carved in stone ON the temple's inner walls

Was there a basin instead of the floor?
I think there was a basin instead of the floor
the Paradise-self sits ON raised floor/time
IN a star-and-tax haven
no specific time

possibly Thrown OUT . Due to CRIME
Everyone feels the night air on their KIND
after which permission is granted to keep and maintain

we must find the right park, the castle
where all rooms have at least two doors, where
all vessels are connected !!

(slough, poison) has thrown OUT
the key to life and death . Due to CRIME
I had hoverflies carved OUT
The Key
DeaTH

in quiry's lonely lair

A stone i have carved OUT
Remembering.
the place of creation.

i was GIVEN PERMISSION
i sit outboard WITH the motor

All vessels are connected
the garden in the inner walls of the temple
The Human Condition
utopia aba The Skin of Time

Aba a utopia, the beginning of Time
Aba a utopia, the End of time

To Attract THE loss
The loss of God's density
Something's density
By Eating the Key

DOD
The Raised floor of. time

he / she / they enjoy the cOOl night air on their cheeks
guarded by cherubim

I enjoy the cool evening air against my garden

a LOST FLOOR

enjoying my cheek's cool evening air

the garden is a place within a place
where history becomes increasingly less of a myth

HYMN

heere is Our, offer
we copy .. ouur bodies
all we Have are blood vessels
twisted silent around the things
THAT dreams are made of,

we copy our blood vessels,
Our language. is habitat for Every thing – else
we will interlace our blood vessels..
with branches of. Blooming. Apple iinto a braid

we make Festoons from our blood vessels,
polished … painted and put . in place..
and let the the. Melted . Icebergs, run
against our DESERT of nondeGradability

so please,
ants, apes, lions, lilies..
have MerCy on US

So Please
ants, apes, lions, lilies,
. the second wwe copy our . lives …

technoscientific6

we need them, the arched rooms
now that we have the castle
we pass through
rivers like wild mirrors

Weeping together,
dancing in windcatchers.
Some keep their eyes in the heart
and you can explode my heart to huge!

Then we get to the door and: blooMing everywhere!

And it appears, you open your mouth: this is Life,
a plant-thing inside me, homeless, lakes, a blue/clear rise..
This is life.

They have a billion Little Big Bangs,
. littleBigs .
LITTLE, can merge together
= to rise, rise, rising, melting together,
EVERYONE can relate
EVERYONE has photos of me
i have photos of EVERYONE,
and those photos, foamy, bubbly photos
are important in order
tto keep it together

And like i said, i mirror lakes,
they will melt,
grow, grow, grow on each other, a blue/clear rise
and because of all these small explosions
they are actually everyone, everything,
everything and everyone

= the sun is YELLOW.

I feel the moon beneath the surface:

Dazzling Space with arched PROMISES

in Eternal Green.

They, AS IN the hearts, BEAT back from all times,
aLL places,
in front of the mirror, completely *homeless,*
NO thing reflected in the mirrors, lakes, souls,
uh,
reflected in the mirrors, lakes, souls:

I dreamt of

Converse men, Women
quite clearly,
sugar peas, Women, what a dream.
A box that you could Buy YOUR WAY INTO.
Big expectations. Big expectations.
RIGHT BEHIND the tent. BEHIND.
i went to today,
we were mega-rich.

I believe anything is possible,
i think we should take this further –
it could lead northward,
that is what i want at this point in time, go north ,
with bright . Nights
and BLack spruce..

all this You start to dream:
Beber Champan de color verde brilliante con sabor lluvia.

An IDEAl party, ALL humans,
i arrive in gold, my gameplay is twitch,

i play it cool, which is a dream
come true, drink champagne
in the eternalgreen . rain.

We have made a decorative orb out of stuff,
and there is an electronic version,
one (or many) theatrical versions
and a physical version in a box
that you can buy and suck on.
oh well. Big expectations.
Big expectations for a . person, who is too old.
NUTS for today!
Drinking eternalgreen.
(to AVOID talking about ANY kind of change).
HANGING OUT BEHIND the tent,
WITHOUT EXCUSING myself.
Brilliantly green.

Inorganically clear!
Mother Yellow light!
Listen!

... also segeln wir durch die Flüsse wie Spiegel ...

wrung / wrong
deploy / deplore

TRANSLATOR'S NOTE

Ursula Andkjær Olsen (b. 1970) made her literary debut in 2000 and has since published nine books of poetry and one novel in addition to several dramatic texts and libretti. She has received numerous accolades for her work, including the prestigious literary award Montanaprisen for her 214-page poem *Det 3. årtusindes hjerte (Third-Millennium Heart)*, from a judging committee who hailed her as "one of the wildest and sharpest intellects in Danish contemporary poetry." In 2015, Olsen's sequel to *Third-Millennium Heart*, a book-length mirror poem titled *Udgående Fartøj (Outgoing Vessel)*, received the Danish Critics Prize for Literature. The judges' statement described the poetic work as "an eruption of anger and a philosophical manifesto, a wail and a hymn, an interrogation of metaphysics, a critique of our age, and a future utopia."

Like *Third-Millennium Heart, Outgoing Vessel* is written as a series of poetic suites that forge one long poem, with a ritualistic repetition of certain lines and images. One literary critic noted in the Danish broadsheet *Politiken*:

> While *Third-Millennium Heart* was about grief and capitalism, *Outgoing Vessel* is about grief and science fiction. The grieving over multiple miscarriages, which gave *Third-Millennium Heart* its wild depth, is still there; however, in *Outgoing Vessel*, grief has become a hard orb, hidden far inside the speaker's 'distant interior.' In there, utopian hopes of change loom.

Compared to *Third-Millennium Heart*, the pleasures and perils of translating *Outgoing Vessel* have been similar in terms of rendering Olsen's many cultural references and infamous experiments with puns, syntax, and neologisms. While I had to produce solutions to these challenges case-by-case, my goal was always to bring forward the jarring quality of the original text in an attempt to create new poetic possibilities in the meeting between languages. For instance, instead of translating *forvredethed* as "distortion" or "twistedness" I decided on "wrungness" for the following lines: "i have wrung myself to create / the necessary loop / wrungness caused by external violence / wrungness caused by the exercise of violence / wrungness caused by flight / wrungness caused by care."

I created this neologism to preserve the uncanny play on "wrung" that exists in the Danish version, which, to me, is the highlight of the poem. Aside from the visceral image that "wrungness" evokes in the context of this poem, I like the way it echoes "wrongness," adding another layer of meaning to the evolution of the poem in translation.

In another poem, *den ukrænkeligste / urørligste* becomes "the sacrosanctest / untouchablest" in my translation, while in a third, *jeg er et æsel som skal skamrides / jeg er et dyr som skal elskes skamløst af de skamløse* becomes "i am a donkey that must be shameridden / i am an animal that must be loved shamelessly / by the shameless." The choice to directly mistranslate the Danish word *skamrides* to "shameridden" instead of 'accurately' translating the word to "overridden" was informed by the context of the word: in order to preserve the play on shame in the original couplet, I chose to insert a neologism in English instead of 'overriding' the image with a more correct translation. I also felt the line became too long in English and read better with an extra break. Thus, the couplet becomes a tercet in my translation. In general, I would prioritize readability and new opportunities for word play in the English version over preserving the original line breaks.

In addition to the challenges mentioned, *Outgoing Vessel's* "technoscientific" poems at the end of each poetic suite introduced further trials in translation. Olsen created these poems by piecing together lines from each suite, running the text through multiple languages in Google Translate, translating it back into Danish via Google Translate, and finally creating a cut-up poem from a long document containing all the various versions of the text. In contrast to the hard, closed voice of the speaker in most of *Outgoing Vessel*, the technoscientific poems unravel throughout the work, becoming increasingly fragmented and open-ended. As a human translator, I knew I had to resist the urge to "clean up" this lack of cohesion. However, a simple method of Google Translating the poems into English turned out to produce aesthetically underwhelming results; after all, while the lines of the poems had been generated by a machine, they had been arranged by a human poet. Consequently, I found myself having to embody a neural machine translation service, become a vessel, in order to capture the cyborg voice of Olsen's human-machine experimentations. The result in translation is an oxymoron: a combination of my logical human self and my chaotic machine self.

As with *Third-Millennium Heart*, my fidelity as the translator of *Outgoing Vessel* lies with the aesthetic spirit of the work rather than the exact content of its Danish sibling. I wanted to allow the work to mutate in translation, to form an identity of its own in English. Fortunately, this approach aligns with Olsen's own philosophy toward translation: she doesn't see her poetry as original work, but rather a translation of an idea. According to Olsen, she is simply the first translator of the idea, and I am the second.

— Katrine Øgaard Jensen

ACKNOWLEDGMENTS

Thanks to the Danish Arts Foundation for supporting the English translation of *Outgoing Vessel*. To the Action Books editors for their endless support. To Katherine Hedeen and the Kenyon Review Translation Workshop for shaping some of the first poems in translation from this work. To Michelle Johnson and *World Literature Today* as well as Jerrold Shiroma and *Seedings* for publishing early excerpts from the work in English.

Special thanks to Chukwuma Ndulue for his invaluable guidance and feedback, and to Orien Longo for (re-)reading the manuscript in its various stages of evolution.

Thomas Bernhard